POEMS

I Know Why the Caged Bird Sings

Gather Together in My Name

Singin' and Swingin' and Gettin' Merry Like Christmas

The Heart of a Woman

Maya Angelou: Poems

Wouldn't Take Nothing for My Journey Now

I Shall Not Be Moved

Even the Stars Look Lonesome

AND COMING SOON IN PAPERBACK
A Song Flung Up to Heaven

POEMS

Maya Angelou

BANTAM BOOKS
New York   Toronto   London
Sydney   Auckland

MAYA ANGELOU: POEMS
JUST GIVE ME A COOL DRINK OF WATER 'FORE I DIIIE,
OH PRAY MY WINGS ARE GONNA FIT ME WELL,
AND STILL I RISE, SHAKER, WHY DON'T YOU SING?
A Bantam Book / published by arrangement with
Random House, Inc.

PUBLISHING HISTORY

Bantam 3 Volume Mass Market edition / November 1981
Bantam 4 Volume Mass Market edition / February 1986
Bantam Trade Edition / June 1997

JUST GIVE ME A COOL DRINK OF WATER 'FORE I DIIIE was originally published by Random House, Inc., in 1971. Bantam edition published January 1973. All rights reserved under International and Pan-American Copyright Conventions. Copyright © 1971 by Maya Angelou. The following poems were first published in The Poetry of Maya Angelou *and are reprinted by permission of Hirt Music, Inc. Copyright © 1969 by Hirt Music Inc.:* "They Went Home," "The Gamut," "To a Man," "No Loser, No Weeper," "When You Come to Me," "Remembering," "In a Time," "Tears," "The Detached," "To a Husband," "Accident," "Let's Majeste," *or the* "Ego and I," "On Diverse Deviations," "Mourning Grace," "Sounds Like Pearls," "When I Think About Myself," "Letter to an Aspiring Junkie," "Miss Scarlett, Mr. Rhett & Other Latter-Day Saints," "Faces," "To a Freedom Fighter," "Riot: 60's," "No No No No," "Black Ode," "My Guilt," "The Calling of Names," "On Working White Liberals," "Sepia Fashion Show," "The Thirteens (Black)," "The Thirteens (White)," "Harlem Hopscotch"; *OH PRAY MY WINGS ARE GONNA FIT ME WELL was originally published by Random House, Inc., August 1975. Bantam edition published October 1977. Copyright © 1975 by Maya Angelou. Several poems have appeared in* Cosmopolitan *August 1975 and November 1976; AND STILL I RISE was originally published by Random House, Inc., August 1978. Bantam edition published January 1980. Portions of this book appeared in* Cosmopolitan *during 1978 as* "Phenomenal Woman" *and* "Just for a Time." *Copyright © 1978 by Maya Angelou; SHAKER, WHY DON'T YOU SING? was originally published by Random House, Inc., February 1983. Portions of this book appeared in the* Ladies' Home Journal *July 1983 and in* New Woman *September 1985 through December 1985.*

All rights reserved.
Copyright © 1986 by Bantam Books.
Cover photograph copyright © 1997 by Dwight Carter.
Library of Congress Catalog Card Number: 93-5904.
No part of this book may be reproduced or transmitted
in any form or by any means, electronic or mechanical,
including photocopying, recording, or by any information
storage and retrieval system, without permission in writing
from the publisher.
For information address: Random House, Inc.,
201 East 50th Street, New York, NY 10022.

ISBN 0-553-37985-2

Published simultaneously in the United States and Canada

Bantam Books are published by Bantam Books, a division of Random House, Inc. Its trademark, consisting of the words "Bantam Books" and the portrayal of a rooster, is Registered in U.S. Patent and Trademark Office and in other countries. Marca Registrada. Bantam Books, 1540 Broadway, New York, New York 10036.

PRINTED IN THE UNITED STATES OF AMERICA

10   9   8

CONTENTS

OH PRAY MY WINGS ARE GONNA FIT ME WELL

AND STILL I RISE

JUST GIVE ME A COOL DRINK OF WATER 'FORE I DIIIE

to
Amber Sam
and the
Zorro Man

Where Love Is a Scream of Anguish

THEY WENT HOME

They went home and told their wives,
   that never once in all their lives,
   had they known a girl like me,
But . . . They went home.

They said my house was licking clean,
   no word I spoke was ever mean,
   I had an air of mystery,
But . . . They went home.

My praises were on all men's lips,
   they liked my smile, my wit, my hips,
   they'd spend one night, or two or three.
But . . .

she a mistress
who's sleeping w/ men
who leave after a day

THE GAMUT

Soft you day, be velvet soft,
   My true love approaches,
Look you bright, you dusty sun,
   Array your golden coaches.

   Soft you wind, be soft as silk
My true love is speaking.
   Hold you birds, your silver throats,
His golden voice I'm seeking.

Come you death, in haste, do come
   My shroud of black be weaving,
Quiet my heart, be deathly quiet,
   My true love is leaving.

Her love is dying

A ZORRO MAN

Here
in the wombed room
silk purple drapes
flash a light as subtle
as your hands before
love-making

Here
in the covered lens
I catch a
clitoral image of
your general inhabitation
long and like a
late dawn in winter

Here
this clean mirror
traps me unwilling
in a gone time
when I was love
and you were booted and brave
and trembling for me.

TO A MAN

My man is
Black Golden Amber
Changing.
Warm mouths of Brandy Fine
Cautious sunlight on a patterned rug
Coughing laughter, rocked on a whorl of French
   tobacco
Graceful turns on woolen stilts
Secretive?
A cat's eye.
Southern. Plump and tender with navy bean
   sullenness
And did I say "Tender"?
The gentleness
A big cat stalks through stubborn bush
And did I mention "Amber"?
The heatless fire consuming itself.
Again. Anew. Into ever neverlessness.
My man is Amber
Changing
Always into itself
New. Now New.
Still itself.
Still.

Describing her love

LATE OCTOBER

Carefully
the leaves of autumn
sprinkle down the tinny
sound of little dyings
and skies sated
of ruddy sunsets
of roseate dawns
roil ceaselessly in
cobweb greys and turn
to black
for comfort.

Only lovers
see the fall
a signal end to endings
a gruffish gesture alerting
those who will not be alarmed
that we begin to stop
in order simply
to begin
again.

describing autumn

NO LOSER, NO WEEPER

"I hate to lose something,"
    then she bent her head
"even a dime, I wish I was dead.
I can't explain it. No more to be said.
Cept I hate to lose something."

"I lost a doll once and cried for a week.
She could open her eyes, and do all but speak.
I believe she was took, by some doll-snatching-
    sneak
I tell you, I hate to lose something."

"A watch of mine once, got up and walked away.
It had twelve numbers on it and for the time of
    day.
I'll never forget it and all I can say
Is I really hate to lose something."

"Now if I felt that way about a watch and a toy,
What you think I feel bout my lover-boy?
I ain't threatening you madam, but he is my
    evening's joy.
And I mean I really hate to lose something."

WHEN YOU COME TO ME

When you come to me, unbidden,
Beckoning me
    To long-ago rooms,
Where memories lie.

    Offering me, as to a child, an attic,
Gatherings of days too few.
    Baubles of stolen kisses.
Trinkets of borrowed loves.
    Trunks of secret words,
                    I CRY.

REMEMBERING

Soft grey ghosts crawl up my sleeve
to peer into my eyes
while I within deny their threats
and answer them with lies.

Mushlike memories perform
a ritual on my lips
I lie in stolid hopelessness
and they lay my soul in strips.

IN A TIME

In a time of secret wooing
Today prepares tomorrow's ruin
Left knows not what right is doing
My heart is torn asunder.

In a time of furtive sighs
Sweet hellos and sad goodbyes
Half-truths told and entire lies
My conscience echoes thunder

In a time when kingdoms come
Joy is brief as summer's fun
Happiness, its race has run
Then pain stalks in to plunder.

TEARS

Tears
The crystal rags
Viscous tatters
of a worn-through soul

Moans
Deep swan song
Blue farewell
of a dying dream.

THE DETACHED

We die,
Welcoming Bluebeards to our darkening closets,
Stranglers to our outstretched necks.
     Stranglers, who neither care nor
     care to know that
     DEATH IS INTERNAL.

We pray,
Savoring sweet the teethed lies,
Bellying the grounds before alien gods
     Gods, who neither know nor
     wish to know that
     HELL IS INTERNAL.

We love,
Rubbing the nakednesses with gloved hands
Inverting our mouths in tongued kisses,
     Kisses that neither touch nor
     care to touch if
     LOVE IS INTERNAL.

TO A HUSBAND

Your voice at times a fist
    Tight in your throat
Jabs ceaselessly at phantoms
    In the room,
Your hand a carved and
    skimming boat
Goes down the Nile
    To point out Pharaoh's tomb.

You're Africa to me
    At brightest dawn.
The Congo's green and
    Copper's brackish hue,
A continent to build
    With Black Man's brawn.
I sit at home and see it all
    Through you.

ACCIDENT

tonight
   when you spread your pallet
of magic,
   I escaped.
sitting apart,
   I saw you grim and unkempt.
Your vulgar-ness
   not of living
your demands
   not from need.

tonight
   as you sprinkled your brain-dust
of rainbows,
   I had no eyes.
Seeing all
I saw the colors fade
and change.
   The blood, red dulled
through the dyes,
and the naked
Black-White truth.

LET'S MAJESTE

I sit a throne upon the times
when Kings are rare and
Consorts
slide into the grease of scullery maids.

So gaily wave a crown of light
(astride the royal chair) that blinds
the commoners who genuflect and cross their
    fingers.

The years will lie beside me
on the queenly bed.
And coupled we'll await
the ages' dust to cake my lids again.

And when the rousing kiss is given,
why must it always be a fairy, and
only just a Prince?

AFTER

No sound falls
from the moaning sky
No scowl wrinkles
the evening pool
    The stars lean down
    A stony brilliance
    While birds fly

The market leers
its empty shelves
Streets bare bosoms
to scanty cars
    This bed yawns
    beneath the weight
    of our absent selves.

THE MOTHERING BLACKNESS

She came home running
   back to the mothering blackness
   deep in the smothering blackness
white tears icicle gold plains of her face
   She came home running

She came down creeping
   here to the black arms waiting
   now to the warm heart waiting
rime of alien dreams befrost her rich brown face
   She came down creeping

She came home blameless
   black yet as Hagar's daughter
   tall as was Sheba's daughter
threats of northern winds die on the desert's face
   She came home blameless

ON DIVERSE DEVIATIONS

When love is a shimmering curtain
Before a door of chance
That leads to a world in question
Wherein the macabrous dance
Of bones that rattle in silence
Of blinded eyes and rolls
Of thick lips thin, denying
A thousand powdered moles,
Where touch to touch is feel
And life a weary whore
    I would be carried off, not gently
    To a shore,
    Where love is the scream of anguish
    And no curtain drapes the door.

MOURNING GRACE

If today, I follow death
go down its trackless wastes,
salt my tongue on hardened tears
for my precious dear times waste
race
along that promised cave in a headlong
deadlong
haste,
Will you
have
the
grace
to mourn for
me?

HOW I CAN LIE TO YOU

now thread my voice
with lies
of lightness
force within
my mirror eyes
the cold disguise
of sad and wise
decisions.

SOUNDS LIKE PEARLS

Sounds
  Like pearls
Roll off your tongue
  To grace this eager ebon ear.

Doubt and fear,
  Ungainly things,
With blushings
  Disappear.

PART TWO

Just Before the World Ends

WHEN I THINK ABOUT MYSELF

When I think about myself,
I almost laugh myself to death,
My life has been one great big joke,
A dance that's walked
A song that's spoke,
I laugh so hard I almost choke
When I think about myself.

Sixty years in these folks' world
The child I works for calls me girl
I say "Yes ma'am" for working's sake.
Too proud to bend
Too poor to break,
I laugh until my stomach ache,
When I think about myself.

My folks can make me split my side,
I laughed so hard I nearly died,
The tales they tell, sound just like lying,
They grow the fruit,
But eat the rind,
I laugh until I start to crying,
When I think about my folks.

ON A BRIGHT DAY,
NEXT WEEK

On a bright day, next week
Just before the bomb falls
Just before the world ends,
   Just before I die

All my tears will powder
Black in dust like ashes
Black like Buddha's belly
   Black and hot and dry

Then will mercy tumble
Falling down in godheads
Falling on the children
   Falling from the sky

LETTER TO AN ASPIRING
JUNKIE

Let me hip you to the streets,
Jim,
Ain't nothing happening.
Maybe some tomorrows gone up in smoke,
raggedy preachers, telling a joke
to lonely, son-less old ladies' maids.

Nothing happening,
Nothing shakin', Jim.
A slough of young cats riding that
cold, white horse,
a grey old monkey on their back, of course
does rodeo tricks.

No haps, man.
No haps.
A worn-out pimp, with a space-age conk,
setting up some fool for a game of tonk,
or poker or
get 'em dead and alive.

The streets?
Climb into the streets man, like you climb
into the ass end of a lion.
Then it's fine.
It's a bug-a-loo and a shing-a-ling,
African dreams on a buck-and-a-wing and a
    prayer.
That's the streets man,
Nothing happening.

MISS SCARLETT,
MR. RHETT AND OTHER
LATTER-DAY SAINTS

———————— ≈ ————————

Novitiates sing Ave
Before the whipping posts,
Criss-crossing their breasts and
tear-stained robes
in the yielding dark.

Animated by the human sacrifice
(Golgotha in black-face)
Priests glow purely white on the
bas-relief of a plantation shrine.

(O Sing)
You are gone but not forgotten
Hail, Scarlett. Requiescat in pace.

God-Makers smear brushes in
blood/gall
to etch frescoes on your
ceilinged tomb.

(O Sing)
Hosanna, King Kotton.

Shadowed couplings of infidels
tempt stigmata from the nipples
of your true-believers.

(Chant Maternoster)
Hallowed Little Eva.

Ministers make novena with the
charred bones of four
very small
very black
very young children

(Intone DIXIE)

And guard the relics
of your intact hymen
daily putting to death,
into eternity,
The stud, his seed,
His seed
His seed.

(O Sing)
Hallelujah, pure Scarlett
Blessed Rhett, the Martyr.

TIMES-SQUARE-
SHOESHINE-COMPOSITION

I'm the best that ever done it
(pow pow)
    that's my title and I won it
    (pow pow)
I ain't lying, I'm the best
(pow pow)
    Come and put me to the test
    (pow pow)

I'll clean 'em till they squeak
(pow pow)
    In the middle of next week,
    (pow pow)
I'll shine 'em till they whine
(pow pow)
    Till they call me master mine
    (pow pow)

For a quarter and a dime
(pow pow)
    You can get the dee luxe shine
    (pow pow)
Say you wanta pay a quarter?
(pow pow)
    Then you give that to your daughter
    (pow pow)

I ain't playing dozens mister
(pow pow)
    You can give it to your sister
    (pow pow)
Any way you want to read it
(pow pow)
    Maybe it's your momma need it.
    (pow pow)

Say I'm like a greedy bigot,
(pow pow)
    I'm a cap'tilist, can you dig it?
    (pow pow)

FACES

Faces and more remember
then reject
the brown caramel days of youth
Reject the sun-sucked tit of
childhood mornings.
Poke a muzzle of war in the trust frozen eyes
                    of a favored doll
Breathe, Brother
and displace a moment's hate with organized
    love.
A poet screams "CHRIST WAITS AT THE
    SUBWAY!"
But who sees?

TO A FREEDOM FIGHTER

You drink a bitter draught.
I sip the tears your eyes fight to hold
A cup of lees, of henbane steeped in chaff.
Your breast is hot,
Your anger black and cold,
Through evening's rest, you dream
I hear the moans, you die a thousands' death.
When cane straps flog the body
dark and lean, you feel the blow,
I hear it in your breath.

RIOT: 60'S

Our
YOUR FRIEND CHARLIE pawnshop
was a glorious blaze
I heard the flames lick
then eat the trays
of zircons
mounted in red gold alloys

Easter clothes and stolen furs
burned in the attic
radios and teevees
crackled with static
plugged in
only to a racial outlet

Some
thought the FRIENDLY FINANCE FURNITURE
    CO.
burned higher
When a leopard print sofa with gold legs
(which makes into a bed)
caught fire
an admiring groan from the waiting horde
"Absentee landlord
you got that shit"

Lighting: a hundred Watts
Detroit, Newark and New York
Screeching nerves, exploding minds
lives tied to
a policeman's whistle
a welfare worker's doorbell
finger.

Hospitality, southern-style
corn pone grits and you-all smile
whole blocks novae
brand new stars
policemen caught in their
brand new cars
Chugga chugga chigga
git me one nigga
lootin' n burnin'
he won't git far

Watermelons, summer ripe
grey neck bones and boiling tripe
supermarket roastin like the
noon-day sun
national guard nervous with his shiny gun
goose the motor quicker
here's my nigga picka
shoot him in the belly
shoot him while he run.

WE SAW BEYOND OUR
SEEMING

We saw beyond our seeming
    These days of bloodied screaming

Of children dying bloated
    Out where the lilies floated

Of men all noosed and dangling
    Within the temples strangling

Our guilt grey fungus growing
    We knew and lied our knowing

Deafened and unwilling
    We aided in the killing

And now our souls lie broken
    Dry tablets without token.

BLACK ODE

Your beauty is a thunder
and I am set a wandering—a wandering
Deafened
Down twilight tin-can alleys
And moist sounds
"OOo wee Baby, Look what you could get if your
    name

                                    was Willie"
Oh, to dip your words like snuff.

A laughter, black and streaming
And I am come a being—a being
Rounded
Up Baptist, aisles, so moaning
And moist sounds
"Bless her heart. Take your bed and walk.
                    You been heavy burdened"
Oh, to lick your love like tears.

NO NO NO NO

No
the two legg'd beasts
that walk like men
play stink finger in their crusty asses
while crackling babies
in napalm coats
stretch mouths to receive
burning tears
on splitting tongues
JUST GIVE ME A COOL DRINK OF WATER
   'FORE I DIIIE

No
the gap legg'd whore
of the eastern shore
enticing Europe to COME
in her
and turn her pigeon shit back to me
to me
Who stoked the coal that drove the ships
which brought her over the sinuous cemetery
Of my many brothers

No
the cocktailed after noons
of what can I do.
In my white layed pink world
I've let your men cram my mouth
with their black throbbing hate
and I swallowed after
I've let your mammies
steal from my kitchens
(I was always half-amused)
I've chuckled the chins of
your topsy-haired pickaninnies.
What more can I do?
I'll never be black like you.
(HALLELUJAH)

No
the red-shoed priests riding
palanquined
in barefoot children country.
The plastered saints gazing down
beneficently
on kneeling mothers
picking undigested beans
from yesterday's shit.

I have waited
toes curled, hat rolled
heart and genitals
in hand
on the back porches
of forever
in the kitchens and fields
of rejections
on the cold marble steps
of America's White Out-House
in the drop seats of buses
and the open flies of war

No more
the dream that you
will cease haunting me
down in fetid swamps of fear
and will turn to embrace your own
humanity
which I AM

No more
The hope that
the razored insults
which mercury slide over your tongue
will be forgotten
and you will learn the words of love
Mother Brother Father Sister Lover Friend

My hopes
dying slowly
rose petals falling
beneath an autumn red moon
will not adorn your unmarked graves

My dreams
lying quietly
a dark pool under the trees
will not carry your name
to a forgetful shore
And what a pity

What a pity
That pity has folded in upon itself
an old man's mouth
whose teeth are gone
and I have no pity.

MY GUILT

My guilt is "slavery's chains," too long
the clang of iron falls down the years.
This brother's sold. This sister's gone
is bitter wax, lining my ears.
My guilt made music with the tears.

My crime is "heroes, dead and gone"
dead Vesey, Turner, Gabriel,
dead Malcolm, Marcus, Martin King.
They fought too hard, they loved too well.
My crime is I'm alive to tell.

My sin is "hanging from a tree"
I do not scream, it makes me proud.
I take to dying like a man.
I do it to impress the crowd.
My sin lies in not screaming loud.

THE CALLING OF NAMES

He went to being called a Colored man
after answering to "hey nigger,"
Now that's a big jump,
anyway you figger,
      Hey, Baby, Watch my smoke.
From colored man to Negro
With the N in caps,
was like saying Japanese
instead of saying Japs.
      I mean, during the war.
The next big step
was a change for true,
From Negro in caps
to being a Jew.
      Now, Sing Yiddish Mama.
Light, Yellow, Brown
and Dark brown skin,
were o.k. colors to
describe him then,
      He was a Bouquet of Roses.
He changed his seasons
like an almanac,
Now you'll get hurt
if you don't call him "Black."
      Nigguh, I ain't playin' this time.

ON WORKING WHITE
LIBERALS

I don't ask the Foreign Legion
Or anyone to win my freedom
Or to fight my battle better than I can,

Though there's one thing that I cry for
I believe enough to die for
That is every man's responsibility to man.

I'm afraid they'll have to prove first
that they'll watch the Black man move first
Then follow him with faith to kingdom come,
This rocky road is not paved for us,
So, I'll believe in Liberal's aid for us
When I see a white man load a Black man's gun.

SEPIA FASHION SHOW

Their hair, pomaded, faces jaded
bones protruding, hip-wise,
The models strutted, backed and butted,
Then stuck their mouths out, lip-wise.

They'd nasty manners, held like banners,
while they looked down their nose-wise,
I'd see 'em in hell, before they'd sell
me one thing they're wearing, clothes-wise.

The Black Bourgeois, who all say "yah"
When yeah is what they're meaning
Should look around, both up and down
before they set out preening.

"Indeed" they swear, "that's what I'll wear
When I go country-clubbing,"
I'd remind them please, look at those knees
you got a Miss Ann's scrubbing.

THE THIRTEENS (BLACK)

Your Momma took to shouting
Your Poppa's gone to war,
Your sister's in the streets
Your brother's in the bar,
The thirteens. Right On.

Your cousin's taking smack
Your Uncle's in the joint,
Your buddy's in the gutter
Shooting for his point
The thirteens. Right On.

And you, you make me sorry
You out here by yourself,
I'd call you something dirty,
But there just ain't nothing left,
cept
The thirteens. Right On.

THE THIRTEENS (WHITE)

Your Momma kissed the chauffeur,
Your Poppa balled the cook,
Your sister did the dirty,
in the middle of the book,
The thirteens. Right On.

Your daughter wears a jock strap,
Your son he wears a bra
Your brother jonesed your cousin
in the back seat of the car.
The thirteens. Right On.

Your money thinks you're something
But if I'd learned to curse,
I'd tell you what your name is
But there just ain't nothing worse
than
The thirteens. Right On.

HARLEM HOPSCOTCH

One foot down, then hop! It's hot.
  Good things for the ones that's got.
Another jump, now to the left.
  Everybody for hisself.

In the air, now both feet down.
  Since you black, don't stick around.
Food is gone, the rent is due,
  Curse and cry and then jump two.

All the people out of work,
  Hold for three, then twist and jerk.
Cross the line, they count you out.
  That's what hopping's all about.

Both feet flat, the game is done.
They think I lost. I think I won.

OH PRAY MY WINGS
ARE GONNA
FIT ME WELL

———————— ❧ ————————

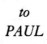

to
PAUL

PART ONE

PICKIN EM UP
AND LAYIN EM DOWN

There's a long-legged girl
in San Francisco
by the Golden Gate.
She said she'd give me all I wanted
but I just couldn't wait.
I started to
Pickin em up
        and layin em down,
Pickin em up
        and layin em down,
Pickin em up
        and layin em down,
gettin to the next town
Baby.

There's a pretty brown
in Birmingham
Boys, she little and cute
but when she like to tied me down
I had to grab my suit and started to
Pickin em up
        and layin em down,
Pickin em up
        and layin em down,
Pickin em up
        and layin em down,
gettin to the next town
Baby.

I met that lovely Detroit lady
and thought my time had come
But just before I said "I do"
I said "I got to run" and started to
Pickin em up
          and layin em down,
Pickin em up
          and layin em down,
Pickin em up
          and layin em down,
gettin to the next town
Baby.

There ain't no words for what I feel
about a pretty face
But if I stay I just might miss
a prettier one some place
I start to
Pickin em up
          and layin em down,
Pickin em up
          and layin em down,
Pickin em up
          and layin em down,
gettin to the next town
Baby.

HERE'S TO ADHERING

I went to a party
   out in Hollywood,
The atmosphere was shoddy
   but the drinks were good,
     and that's where I heard you laugh.

I then went cruising
   on an old Greek ship,
The crew was amusing
   but the guests weren't hip,
     that's where I found your hands.

On to the Sahara
   in a caravan,
The sun struck like an arrow
   but the nights were grand,
     and that's how I found your chest.

An evening in the Congo
   where the Congo ends,
I found myself alone, oh
   but I made some friends,
     that's where I saw your face.

I have been devoting
   all my time to get
Parts of you out floating
   still unglued as yet.

Won't you pull yourself together

For

  Me

ONCE

ON REACHING FORTY

Other acquainted years
sidle
with modest
decorum
across the scrim of toughened
tears and to a stage
planked with laughter boards
and waxed with rueful loss
But forty
with the authorized
brazenness of a uniformed
cop stomps
no-knocking
into the script
bumps a funky grind on the
shabby curtain of youth
and delays the action.

Unless you have the inborn
wisdom
and grace
and are clever enough
to die at
thirty-nine.

THE TELEPHONE

It comes in black
and blue, indecisive
beige. In red and chaperons my life.
Sitting like a strict
and spinstered Aunt
spiked between my needs
and need.

It tats the day, crocheting
other people's lives
in neat arrangements
ignoring me
busy with the hemming
of strangers' overlong affairs or
the darning of my
neighbors' worn-out
dreams.

From Monday, the morning of the week,
through mid-times
noon and Sunday's dying
light. It sits silent.
Its needle sound
does not transfix my ear
or draw my longing to
a close.

Ring. Damn you!

PART TWO

PASSING TIME

Your skin like dawn
Mine like dusk.

One paints the beginning
of a certain end.

The other, the end of a
sure beginning.

NOW LONG AGO

One innocent spring
your voice meant to me
less than tires turning
on a distant street.

Your name, perhaps spoken,
led no chorus of
batons
unrehearsed
to crush against my
empty chest.

That cool spring
was shortened by
your summer, bold impatient
and all forgotten
except when silence
turns the key
into my midnight bedroom
and comes to sleep upon your
pillow.

GREYDAY

The day hangs heavy
loose and grey
when you're away.

A crown of thorns
a shirt of hair
is what I wear.

No one knows
my lonely heart
when we're apart.

POOR GIRL

You've got another love
  and I know it
Someone who adores you
  just like me
Hanging on your words
  like they were gold
Thinking that she understands
  your soul
Poor Girl
    Just like me.

You're breaking another heart
  and I know it
And there's nothing
  I can do
If I try to tell her
  what I know
She'll misunderstand
  and make me go
Poor Girl
    Just like me.

You're going to leave her too
  and I know it
She'll never know
  what made you go
She'll cry and wonder
  what went wrong

Then she'll begin
    to sing this song
Poor Girl
        Just like me.

COME, AND BE MY BABY

The highway is full of big cars
going nowhere fast
And folks is smoking anything that'll burn
Some people wrap their lives around a cocktail
    glass
And you sit wondering
where you're going to turn
I got it.
Come. And be my baby.

Some prophets say the world is gonna end
    tomorrow
But others say we've got a week or two
The paper is full of every kind of blooming
    horror
And you sit wondering
What you're gonna do.
I got it.
Come. And be my baby.

SENSES OF INSECURITY

I couldn't tell fact from fiction
  or if my dream was true,
The only sure prediction
  in this whole world was you.
I'd touched your features inchly
  heard love and dared the cost.
The scented spiel reeled me unreal
  and found my senses lost.

ALONE

Lying, thinking
Last night
How to find my soul a home
Where water is not thirsty
And bread loaf is not stone
I came up with one thing
And I don't believe I'm wrong
That nobody,
But nobody
Can make it out here alone.

Alone, all alone
Nobody, but nobody
Can make it out here alone.

There are some millionaires
With money they can't use
Their wives run round like banshees
Their children sing the blues
They've got expensive doctors
To cure their hearts of stone.
But nobody
No nobody
Can make it out here alone.

Alone, all alone
Nobody, but nobody
Can make it out here alone.

Now if you listen closely
I'll tell you what I know
Storm clouds are gathering
The wind is gonna blow
The race of man is suffering
And I can hear the moan,
Cause nobody,
But nobody
Can make it out here alone.

Alone, all alone
Nobody, but nobody
Can make it out here alone.

COMMUNICATION I

She wished of him a lover's kiss and
nights of coupled twining
They laced themselves
between the trees
and to the water's edge.

Reminding her
the cratered moon lay light years away
he spoke of Greece, the Parthenon
and Cleopatra's barge.

She splayed her foot
up to the shin
within the ocean brine.

He quoted Pope and Bernard Shaw
and Catcher in the Rye.

Her sandal lost
she dried her toe
and then she mopped her brow.

Dry-eyed
she walked into her room
and frankly told her mother
"Of all he said I understood,
he said he loved another."

COMMUNICATION II

for Adele

The Student

The dust of ancient pages
had never touched his face,
and fountains black and comely
were mummyied in a place
beyond
his young un-knowing.

The Teacher

She shared the lettered strivings
of etched Pharaonic walls
and Reconstruction's anguish
resounded down the halls
of all her
dry dreams.

WONDER

A day
drunk with the nectar of
nowness
weaves its way between
the years
to find itself at the flophouse
of night
to sleep and be seen
no more.

Will I be less
dead because I wrote this
poem or you more because
you read it
long years hence.

A CONCEIT

Give me your hand

Make room for me
to lead and follow
you
beyond this rage of poetry.

Let others have
the privacy of
touching words
and love of loss
of love.

For me
Give me your hand.

PART THREE

REQUEST

If this country is a bastard
will the lowdown mother user
who ran off
and left the woman
moaning in her
green delivery
please come back and claim
his love child.
Give a legal name to beg from
for the first
time of its life.

AFRICA

Thus she had lain
sugar cane sweet
deserts her hair
golden her feet
mountains her breasts
two Niles her tears
Thus she has lain
Black through the years.

Over the white seas
rime white and cold
brigands ungentled
icicle bold
took her young daughters
sold her strong sons
churched her with Jesus
bled her with guns.
Thus she has lain.

Now she is rising
remember her pain
remember the losses
her screams loud and vain
remember her riches
her history slain
now she is striding
although she had lain.

AMERICA

The gold of her promise
    has never been mined

Her borders of justice
    not clearly defined

Her crops of abundance
    the fruit and the grain

Have not fed the hungry
    nor eased that deep pain

Her proud declarations
    are leaves on the wind

Her southern exposure
    black death did befriend

Discover this country
    dead centuries cry

Erect noble tablets
    where none can decry

"She kills her bright future
    and rapes for a sou

Then entraps her children
   with legends untrue"

I beg you

Discover this country.

FOR US,
WHO DARE NOT DARE

Be me a Pharaoh
Build me high pyramids of stone and question
See me the Nile
at twilight
and jaguars moving to
the slow cold draught.

Swim me Congo
Hear me the tails of alligators
flapping waves that reach
a yester shore.

Swing me vines, beyond that Bao-Bab tree,
and talk me chief
Sing me birds
flash color lightening through bright green
     leaves.

Taste me fruit
its juice free falling from
a mother tree.

Know me

Africa.

LORD, IN MY HEART

for Countee Cullen

Holy haloes
   Ring me round

Spirit waves on
   Spirit sound

Meshach and
   Abednego

Golden chariot
   Swinging low

I recite them
   in my sleep

Jordan's cold
   and briny deep

Bible lessons
   Sunday school

Bow before the
   Golden Rule

Now I wonder
   If I tried

Could I turn my
  cheek aside

Marvelling with
  afterthought

Let the blow fall
  saying naught

Of my true Christ-
  like control

and the nature
  of my soul.

Would I strike with
  rage divine

Till the culprit
  fell supine

Hit out broad all
  fury red

Till my foes are
  fallen dead

Teachers of my
  early youth

Taught forgiveness
  stressed the truth

Here then is my
　　Christian lack:

If I'm struck then
　　I'll strike back.

ARTFUL POSE

Of falling leaves and melting
snows, of birds
in their delights
Some poets sing
their melodies
tendering my nights
sweetly.

My pencil halts
and will not go
along that quiet path
I need to write
of lovers false

and hate
and hateful wrath
quickly.

PART FOUR

THE COUPLE

Discard the fear and what
was she? of rag and bones
a mimicry of woman's
fairy ness
Archaic at its birth

Discharge the hate and when
was he? disheveled moans
a mimesis of man's
estate
deceited for its worth

Dissolve the greed and why
were they? enfeebled thrones
a memory of mortal
kindliness
exiled from this earth.

THE PUSHER

He bad
O he bad
He make a honky
poot. Make a honky's
blue eyes squint
anus tight, when
my man look in
the light blue eyes.

He thinks
He don't play
His Afro crown raises
eyes. Raises eyebrows
of wonder and dark
envy when he, combed
out, hits the street.

He sleek
Dashiki
Wax printed on his skin
remembrances of Congo dawns
laced across his chest.
Red Blood Red and Black.

He bought
O He got
Malcolm's paper
back. Checked out the
photo, caught a few godly
lines. Then wondered how
many wives/daughters of
Honky (miscalled The Man)
bird snake
caught, dug them both.
(Him, Fro-ed Dashiki-ed
and the book.)

He stashed
He stands stashed
Near, too near the MLK
Library. P.S. naught
naught naught. Breathing
slaughter on the Malcolm X
Institute. Whole fist
balled, fingers pressing
palm. Shooting up through
Honky's blue-eyed sky.

     "BLACK IS!"
     "NATION TIME!"
     "TOMORROW'S GLORY HERE TODAY"

Pry free the hand
Observe our Black present.
There lie soft on that
copper palm, a death of
coke. A kill of horse
eternal night's barbiturates.
One hundred youths
sped down to
Speed.

He right
O he bad
He badder than death
yet gives no sweet
release.

CHICKEN-LICKEN

She was afraid of men,
sin and the humors
of the night.
When she saw a bed
locks clicked
in her brain.

She screwed a frown
around and plugged
it in the keyhole.
Put a chain across
her door and closed
her mind.

Her bones were found
round thirty years later
when they razed
her building to
put up a parking lot.

Autopsy: read
dead of acute peoplelessness.

PART FIVE

I ALMOST REMEMBER

I almost remember
    smiling some
years past
    even combing the ceiling
with the teeth of a laugh
(longer ago than the
                smile).
Open night news-eyed I watch
channels of hunger
    written on children's faces
    bursting bellies balloon
in the air of my day room.

There was a smile, I recall
now jelled in
a never yester glow. Even a laugh
that tickled the tits of
heaven
(older than the smile).
In graphs, afraid, I see the black
brown hands and
white thin yellowed fingers.

Slip slipping from the
ledge of life. Forgotten by
all but hatred.
Ignored
by all but disdain.

On late evenings when
quiet inhabits my garden
when grass sleeps and
streets are only paths for silent
mist.

I seem to remember

Smiling.

PRISONER

Even sunlight dares
and trembles through
my bars
to shimmer
dances on
the floor.
A clang of
lock and
keys and heels
and blood-dried
guns.
Even sunshine
dares.

It's jail
   and bail
then rails to run.

Guard grey men
serve plates of rattle
noise and concrete
death and beans
Then pale sun stumbles
through the poles of
iron to warm the horror
of grey guard men.

It's jail
    and bail
then rails to run.

Black night. The me
myself of me sleeks
in the folds and history
of fear. To secret hold
me deep and close my
ears of lulls and clangs
and memory of hate.
Then night and sleep
and dreams.

It's jail
    and bail
then rails to run.

WOMAN ME

Your smile, delicate
rumor of peace.
Deafening revolutions nestle in the
cleavage of
your breasts
Beggar-Kings and red-ringed Priests
seek glory at the meeting
of your thighs
A grasp of Lions, A lap of Lambs.

Your tears, jeweled
strewn a diadem
caused Pharaohs to ride
deep in the bosom of the
Nile. Southern spas lash fast
their doors upon the night when
winds of death blow down your name
A bride of hurricanes,
  A swarm of summer wind.

Your laughter, pealing tall
above the bells of ruined cathedrals.
Children reach between your teeth
for charts to live their lives.
A stomp of feet, A bevy of swift hands.

JOHN J.

His soul curdled
standing milk
                    childhood's right gone wrong.

Plum blue, skin brown dusted
eyes black shining,
                    (His momma didn't want him)

The round head slick silk
Turn around, fall down curls
Old ladies smelling of flour
and talcum powder Cashmere Bouquet, said
"This child is pretty enough to be a girl."
                    (But his momma didn't want him)

John J. grinned a "How can you resist me?"
and danced to conjure lightning from
a morning's summer sky.
Gave the teacher an apple kiss
                    (But his momma didn't want him)

His nerves stretched two thousand miles
found a flinging singing lady.
breasting a bar
calling straights on the dice,
gin over ice,

and the 30's version of
everybody in the
pool.

(She didn't want him.)

SOUTHEAST ARKANASIA

After Eli Whitney's gin
brought to generations' end
bartered flesh and broken bones
Did it cleanse you of your sin
   Did you ponder?

Now, when farmers bury wheat
and the cow men dump the sweet
butter down on Davy Jones
Does it sanctify your street
    Do you wonder?

Or is guilt your nightly mare
bucking wake your evenings' share
of the stilled repair of groans
and the absence of despair
      over yonder?

SONG FOR THE OLD ONES

My Fathers sit on benches
   their flesh count every plank
   the slats leave dents of darkness
deep in their withered flanks.

They nod like broken candles
   all waxed and burnt profound,
   they say "It's understanding
that makes the world go round."

There in those pleated faces
   I see the auction block
   the chains and slavery's coffles
the whip and lash and stock.

My Fathers speak in voices
   that shred my fact and sound
   they say "It's our submission
that makes the world go round."

They used the finest cunning
   their naked wits and wiles
   the lowly Uncle Tomming
and Aunt Jemimas' smiles.

They've laughed to shield their crying
   then shuffled through their dreams
   and stepped 'n fetched a country
to write the blues with screams.

I understand their meaning
   it could and did derive
   from living on the edge of death
They kept my race alive.

CHILD DEAD IN OLD SEAS

Father,
I wait for you in oceans
tides washing pyramids high
above my head.
Waves, undulating
corn rows around my
black feet.
The heavens shift and
stars find holes set
new in dark infirmity.
My search goes on.
Dainty shells on ash-like wrists
of debutantes remember you.
Childhood's absence has
not stilled your
voice. My ear
listens. You whisper
on the watery passage.

Deep dirges moan
from the
belly of the sea
and your song
floats to me
of lost savannahs
green and
drums. Of palm trees bending
woman-like swaying

grape-blue children
laugh on beaches
of sand as
white as your bones
clean
on the foot of
long-ago waters.

Father.
I wait for you
wrapped in
the entrails of
whales. Your
blood now
blues
spume
over
the rippled
surface of our
grave.

TAKE TIME OUT

When you see them
on a freeway hitching rides
wearing beads
with packs by their sides
you ought to ask
What's all the
warring and the jarring
and the
killing and
the thrilling
all about.

Take Time Out.

When you see him
with a band around his head
and an army surplus bunk
that makes his bed. You'd
better ask What's
all the
beating and
the cheating and
the bleeding and
the needing
all about.

Take Time Out.

When you see her walking
Barefoot in the rain
And you know she's tripping
on a one-way train
you need to ask
what's all the
lying and the
dying and
the running and
the gunning
all about.

Take Time Out.

Use a minute
feel some sorrow
for the folks
who think tomorrow
is a place that they
can call up
on the phone.
Take a month
and show some kindness
for the folks
who thought that blindness
was an illness that
affected eyes alone.

If you know that youth
is dying on the run
and my daughter trades
dope stories with your son
we'd better see
what all our
fearing and our
jeering and our
crying and
our lying
brought about.

Take Time Out.

ELEGY

———————— ❧ ————————

for Harriet Tubman & Frederick Douglass

I lay down in my grave
and watch my children
grow
Proud blooms
above the weeds of death.

Their petals wave
and still nobody
knows the soft black
dirt that is my winding
sheet. The worms, my friends,
yet tunnel holes in
bones and through those
apertures I see the rain.
The sunfelt warmth
now jabs
within my space and
brings me roots of my
children born.

Their seeds must fall
and press beneath
this earth,
and find me where I

wait. My only need to
fertilize their birth.

I lay down in my grave
and watch my children
grow.

REVERSES

How often must we
    butt to head
Mind to ass
    flank to nuts
    cock to elbow
    hip to toe
    soul to shoulder
    confront ourselves
    in our past.

LITTLE GIRL SPEAKINGS

Ain't nobody better's my Daddy,
   you keep yo' quauter
   I ain't yo' daughter,
Ain't nobody better's my Daddy.

Ain't nothing prettier'n my dollie
   heard what I said,
   don't pat her head,
Ain't nothing prettier'n my dollie.

No lady cookinger than my Mommy
   smell that pie,
   see I don't lie
No lady cookinger than my Mommy.

THIS WINTER DAY

The kitchen is its readiness
white green and orange things
leak their blood selves in the soup.

Ritual sacrifice that snaps
an odor at my nose and starts
my tongue to march
slipping in the liquid of it drip.

The day, silver striped
in rain, is balked against
my window and the soup.

AND STILL
I RISE

This book is dedicated to a
few of the Good Guys

You to laugh with
You to cry to
I can just about make
it over

JESSICA MITFORD
GERARD W. PURCELL
JAY ALLEN

Touch Me, Life, Not Softly

A KIND OF LOVE,
SOME SAY

———— ≫ ————

Is it true the ribs can tell
The kick of a beast from a
Lover's fist? The bruised
Bones recorded well
The sudden shock, the
Hard impact. Then swollen lids,
Sorry eyes, spoke not
Of lost romance, but hurt.

Hate often is confused. Its
Limits are in zones beyond itself. And
Sadists will not learn that
Love by nature, exacts a pain
Unequalled on the rack.

COUNTRY LOVER

Funky blues
Keen toed shoes
High water pants
Saddy night dance
Red soda water
and anybody's daughter

REMEMBRANCE

for Paul

Your hands easy
weight, teasing the bees
hived in my hair, your smile at the
slope of my cheek. On the
occasion, you press
above me, glowing, spouting
readiness, mystery rapes
my reason.

When you have withdrawn
your self and the magic, when
only the smell of your
love lingers between
my breasts, then, only
then, can I greedily consume
your presence.

WHERE WE BELONG, A DUET

In every town and village,
In every city square,
In crowded places
I searched the faces
Hoping to find
Someone to care.

I read mysterious meanings
In the distant stars,
Then I went to schoolrooms
And poolrooms
And half-lighted cocktail bars.
Braving dangers,
Going with strangers,
I don't even remember their names.
I was quick and breezy
And always easy
Playing romantic games.

I wined and dined a thousand exotic Joans and
    Janes
In dusty dance halls, at debutante balls,
On lonely country lanes.
I fell in love forever,
Twice every year or so.
I wooed them sweetly, was theirs completely,
But they always let me go.
Saying bye now, no need to try now,

You don't have the proper charms.
Too sentimental and much too gentle
I don't tremble in your arms.

Then you rose into my life
Like a promised sunrise.
Brightening my days with the light in your eyes.
I've never been so strong,
Now I'm where I belong.

PHENOMENAL WOMAN

Pretty women wonder where my secret lies.
I'm not cute or built to suit a fashion model's size
But when I start to tell them,
They think I'm telling lies.
I say,
It's in the reach of my arms,
The span of my hips,
The stride of my step,
The curl of my lips.
I'm a woman
Phenomenally.
Phenomenal woman,
That's me.

I walk into a room
Just as cool as you please,
And to a man,
The fellows stand or
Fall down on their knees.
Then they swarm around me,
A hive of honey bees.
I say,
It's the fire in my eyes,
And the flash of my teeth,
The swing in my waist,
And the joy in my feet.
I'm a woman
Phenomenally.

Phenomenal woman,
That's me.

Men themselves have wondered
What they see in me.
They try so much
But they can't touch
My inner mystery.
When I try to show them
They say they still can't see.
I say,
It's in the arch of my back,
The sun of my smile,
The ride of my breasts,
The grace of my style.
I'm a woman
Phenomenally.
Phenomenal woman,
That's me.

Now you understand
Just why my head's not bowed.
I don't shout or jump about
Or have to talk real loud.
When you see me passing
It ought to make you proud.
I say,
It's in the click of my heels,
The bend of my hair,
the palm of my hand,
The need for my care.
'Cause I'm a woman
Phenomenally.
Phenomenal woman,
That's me.

MEN

————————— ⬨ —————————

When I was young, I used to
Watch behind the curtains
As men walked up and down
The street. Wino men, old men.
Young men sharp as mustard.
See them. Men are always
Going somewhere.
They knew I was there. Fifteen
Years old and starving for them.
Under my window, they would pause,
Their shoulders high like the
Breasts of a young girl,
Jacket tails slapping over
Those behinds,
Men.

One day they hold you in the
Palms of their hands, gentle, as if you
Were the last raw egg in the world. Then
They tighten up. Just a little. The
First squeeze is nice. A quick hug.
Soft into your defenselessness. A little
More. The hurt begins. Wrench out a
Smile that slides around the fear. When the
Air disappears,
Your mind pops, exploding fiercely, briefly,
Like the head of a kitchen match. Shattered.
It is your juice
That runs down their legs. Staining their shoes.

When the earth rights itself again,
And taste tries to return to the tongue,
Your body has slammed shut. Forever.
No keys exist.

Then the window draws full upon
Your mind. There, just beyond
The sway of curtains, men walk.
Knowing something.
Going someplace.
But this time, you will simply
Stand and watch.

Maybe.

REFUSAL

Beloved,
In what other lives or lands
Have I known your lips
Your hands
Your laughter brave
Irreverent.
Those sweet excesses that
I do adore.
What surety is there
That we will meet again,
On other worlds some
Future time undated.
I defy my body's haste.
Without the Promise
Of one more sweet encounter
I will not deign to die.

JUST FOR A TIME

Oh how you used to walk
With that insouciant smile
I liked to hear you talk
And your style
Pleased me for a while.

You were my early love
New as a day breaking in Spring
You were the image of
Everything
That caused me to sing.

I don't like reminiscing
Nostalgia is not my forté
I don't spill tears
On yesterday's years
But honesty makes me say,
You were a precious pearl
How I loved to see you shine,
You were the perfect girl.
And you were mine.
For a time.
For a time.
Just for a time.

PART TWO

Traveling

JUNKIE MONKEY REEL

Shoulders sag,
The pull of weighted needling.
Arms drag, smacking wet in soft bone
Sockets.

Knees thaw,
Their familiar magic lost. Old bend and
Lock and bend forgot.

Teeth rock in fetid gums.
Eyes dart, die, then float in
Simian juice.

Brains reel,
Master charts of old ideas erased. The
Routes are gone beneath the tracks
Of desert caravans, pre-slavery
Years ago.

Dreams fail,
Unguarded fears on homeward streets
Embrace. Throttling in a dark revenge
Murder is its sweet romance.

How long will
This monkey dance?

THE LESSON

I keep on dying again.
Veins collapse, opening like the
Small fists of sleeping
Children.
Memory of old tombs,
Rotting flesh and worms do
Not convince me against
The challenge. The years
And cold defeat live deep in
Lines along my face.
They dull my eyes, yet
I keep on dying,
Because I love to live.

CALIFORNIA PRODIGAL

for David P-B

The eye follows, the land
Slips upward, creases down, forms
The gentle buttocks of a young
Giant. In the nestle,
Old adobe bricks, washed of
Whiteness, paled to umber,
Await another century.

Star Jasmine and old vines
Lay claim upon the ghosted land,
Then quiet pools whisper
Private childhood secrets.

Flush on inner cottage walls
Antiquitous faces,
Used to the gelid breath
Of old manors, glare disdainfully
Over breached time.

Around and through these
Cold phantasmatalities,
He walks, insisting
To the languid air,
Activity, music,
A generosity of graces.

His lupin fields spurn old
Deceit and agile poppies dance
In golden riot. Each day is
Fulminant, exploding brightly
Under the gaze of his exquisite
Sires, frozen in the famed paint
Of dead masters. Audacious
Sunlight casts defiance
At their feet.

MY ARKANSAS

There is a deep brooding
in Arkansas.
Old crimes like moss pend
from poplar trees.
The sullen earth
is much too
red for comfort.

Sunrise seems to hesitate
and in that second
lose its
incandescent aim, and
dusk no more shadows
than the noon.
The past is brighter yet.

Old hates and
ante-bellum lace, are rent
but not discarded.
Today is yet to come
in Arkansas.
It writhes. It writhes in awful
waves of brooding.

THROUGH THE INNER CITY
TO THE SUBURBS

Secured by sooted windows
And amazement, it is
Delicious. Frosting filched
From a company cake.

People. Black and fast. Scattered
Watermelon seeds on
A summer street. Grinning in
ritual, sassy in pomp.

From a slow moving train
They are precious. Stolen gems
Unsaleable and dear. Those
Dusky undulations sweat of forest
Nights, damp dancing, the juicy
secrets of black thighs.

Images framed picture perfect
Do not move beyond the window
Siding.

Strong delectation:
Dirty stories in changing rooms
Accompany the slap of wet towels and
Toilet seats.
Poli-talk of politician
Parents: "They need shoes and
cooze and a private

warm latrine. I had a colored
Mammy . . ."

The train, bound for green lawns
Double garages and sullen women
in dreaded homes, settles down
On its habit track.
Leaving
The dark figures dancing
And grinning. Still
Grinning.

LADY LUNCHEON CLUB

Her counsel was accepted: the times are grave.
A man was needed who would make them think,
And pay him from the petty cash account.

Our woman checked her golden watch,
The speaker has a plane to catch.
Dessert is served (and just in time).

The lecturer leans, thrusts forth his head
And neck and chest, arms akimbo
On the lectern top. He summons up
Sincerity as one might call a favored
Pet.

He understands the female rage,
Why Eve was lustful and
Delilah's
Grim deceit.

Our woman thinks:
(This cake is much too sweet.)

He sighs for youthful death
And rape at ten, and murder of
The soul stretched over long.

Our woman notes:
(This coffee's much too strong.)

The jobless streets of
Wine and wandering when
Mornings promise no bright relief.

She claps her hands and writes
Upon her pad: (Next time the
Speaker must be brief).

MOMMA WELFARE ROLL

Her arms semaphore fat triangles,
Pudgy hands bunched on layered hips
Where bones idle under years of fatback
And lima beans.
Her jowls shiver in accusation
Of crimes clichéd by
Repetition. Her children, strangers
To childhood's toys, play
Best the games of darkened doorways,
Rooftop tag, and know the slick feel of
Other people's property.

Too fat to whore,
Too mad to work,
Searches her dreams for the
Lucky sign and walks bare-handed
Into a den of bureaucrats for
Her portion.
"They don't give me welfare.
I take it."

THE SINGER WILL NOT SING

for A.L.

A benison given. Unused,
No angels promised,
wings fluttering banal lies
behind their sexlessness. No
trumpets gloried
prophecies of fabled fame.
Yet harmonies waited in
her stiff throat. New notes
lay expectant on her
stilled tongue.

Her lips are ridged and
fleshy. Purpled night birds
snuggled to rest.
The mouth seamed, voiceless,
Sounds do not lift beyond
those reddened walls.

She came too late and lonely
to this place.

WILLIE

Willie was a man without fame
Hardly anybody knew his name.
Crippled and limping, always walking lame,
He said, "I keep on movin'
Movin' just the same."

Solitude was the climate in his head
Emptiness was the partner in his bed,
Pain echoed in the steps of his tread,
He said, "I keep on followin'
Where the leaders led."

I may cry and I will die,
But my spirit is the soul of every spring,
Watch for me and you will see
That I'm present in the songs that children sing.

People called him "Uncle," "Boy" and "Hey,"
Said, "You can't live through this another day."
Then, they waited to hear what he would say.
He said, "I'm living
In the games that children play.

"You may enter my sleep, people my dreams,
Threaten my early morning's ease,
But I keep comin' followin' laughin' cryin',
Sure as a summer breeze.

"Wait for me, watch for me.
My spirit is the surge of open seas.
Look for me, ask for me,
I'm the rustle in the autumn leaves.

"When the sun rises
I am the time.
When the children sing
I am the Rhyme."

TO BEAT THE CHILD WAS BAD ENOUGH

A young body, light
As winter sunshine, a new
Seed's bursting promise,
Hung from a string of silence
Above its future.
(The chance of choice was never known.)
Hunger, new hands, strange voices,
Its cry came natural, tearing.

Water boiled in innocence, gaily
In a cheap pot.
The child exchanged its
Curiosity for terror. The skin
Withdrew, the flesh submitted.

Now, cries make shards
Of broken air, beyond an unremembered
Hunger and the peace of strange hands.

A young body floats.
Silently.

WOMAN WORK

I've got the children to tend
The clothes to mend
The floor to mop
The food to shop
Then the chicken to fry
Then baby to dry
I got company to feed
The garden to weed
I've got the shirts to press
The tots to dress
The cane to be cut
I gotta clean up this hut
Then see about the sick
And the cotton to pick.

Shine on me, sunshine
Rain on me, rain
Fall softly, dewdrops
And cool my brow again.

Storm, blow me from here
With your fiercest wind
Let me float across the sky
'Til I can rest again.

Fall gently, snowflakes
Cover me with white
Cold icy kisses and
Let me rest tonight.

Sun, rain, curving sky
Mountain, oceans, leaf and stone
Star shine, moon glow
You're all that I can call my own.

ONE MORE ROUND

There ain't no pay beneath the sun
As sweet as rest when a job's well done.
I was born to work up to my grave
But I was not born
To be a slave.

One more round
And let's heave it down,
One more round
And let's heave it down.

Papa drove steel and Momma stood guard,
I never heard them holler 'cause the work was
    hard.
They were born to work up to their graves
But they were not born
To be worked-out slaves.

One more round
And let's heave it down,
One more round
And let's heave it down.

Brothers and sisters know the daily grind,
It was not labor made them lose their minds.
They were born to work up to their graves
But they were not born
To be worked-out slaves.

One more round
And let's heave it down,
One more round
And let's heave it down.

And now I'll tell you my Golden Rule,
I was born to work but I ain't no mule.
I was born to work up to my grave
But I was not born
To be a slave.

One more round
And let's heave it down,
One more round
And let's heave it down.

THE TRAVELER

Byways and bygone
And lone nights long
Sun rays and sea waves
And star and stone

Manless and friendless
No cave my home
This is my torture
My long nights, lone

KIN

---

for Bailey

We were entwined in red rings
Of blood and loneliness before
The first snows fell
Before muddy rivers seeded clouds
Above a virgin forest, and
Men ran naked, blue and black
Skinned into the warm embraces
Of Sheba, Eve and Lilith.
I was your sister.

You left me to force strangers
Into brother molds, exacting
Taxations they never
Owed or could ever pay.

You fought to die, thinking
In destruction lies the seed
Of birth. You may be right.

I will remember silent walks in
Southern woods and long talks
In low voices
Shielding meaning from the big ears
Of over-curious adults.

You may be right.
Your slow return from
Regions of terror and bloody

Screams, races my heart.
I hear again the laughter
Of children and see fireflies
Bursting tiny explosion in
An Arkansas twilight.

THE MEMORY

Cotton rows crisscross the world
    And dead-tired nights of yearning
Thunderbolts on leather strops
    And all my body burning

Sugar cane reach up to God
    And every baby crying
Shame the blanket of my night
    And all my days are dying

PART THREE

And Still I Rise

STILL I RISE

You may write me down in history
With your bitter, twisted lies,
You may trod me in the very dirt
But still, like dust, I'll rise.

Does my sassiness upset you?
Why are you beset with gloom?
'Cause I walk like I've got oil wells
Pumping in my living room.

Just like moons and like suns,
With the certainty of tides,
Just like hopes springing high,
Still I'll rise.

Did you want to see me broken?
Bowed head and lowered eyes?
Shoulders falling down like teardrops,
Weakened by my soulful cries.

Does my haughtiness offend you?
Don't you take it awful hard
'Cause I laugh like I've got gold mines
Diggin' in my own back yard.

You may shoot me with your words,
You may cut me with your eyes,

You may kill me with your hatefulness,
But still, like air, I'll rise.

Does my sexiness upset you?
Does it come as a surprise
That I dance like I've got diamonds
At the meeting of my thighs?

Out of the huts of history's shame
I rise
Up from a past that's rooted in pain
I rise
I'm a black ocean, leaping and wide,
Welling and swelling I bear in the tide.

Leaving behind nights of terror and fear
I rise
Into a daybreak that's wondrously clear
I rise
Bringing the gifts that my ancestors gave,
I am the dream and the hope of the slave.
I rise
I rise
I rise.

AIN'T THAT BAD?

Dancin' the funky chicken
Eatin' ribs and tips
Diggin' all the latest sounds
And drinkin' gin in sips.

Puttin' down that do-rag
Tightenin' up my 'fro
Wrappin' up in Blackness
Don't I shine and glow?

Hearin' Stevie Wonder
Cookin' beans and rice
Goin' to the opera
Checkin' out Leontyne Price.

Get down, Jesse Jackson
Dance on, Alvin Ailey
Talk, Miss Barbara Jordan
Groove, Miss Pearlie Bailey.

Now ain't they bad?
An' ain't they Black?
An' ain't they Black?
An' ain't they Bad?
An' ain't they bad?
An' ain't they Black?
An' ain't they fine?

Black like the hour of the night
When your love turns and wriggles close to your
    side
Black as the earth which has given birth
To nations, and when all else is gone will abide.

Bad as the storm that leaps raging from the
    heavens
Bringing the welcome rain
Bad as the sun burning orange hot at midday
Lifting the waters again.

Arthur Ashe on the tennis court
Muhammad Ali in the ring
André Watts and Andrew Young
Black men doing their thing.

Dressing in purples and pinks and greens
Exotic as rum and Cokes
Living our lives with flash and style
Ain't we colorful folks?

Now ain't we bad?
An' ain't we Black?
An' ain't we Black?
An' ain't we bad?
An' ain't we bad?
An' ain't we Black?
An' ain't we fine?

LIFE DOESN'T
FRIGHTEN ME

Shadows on the wall
Noises down the hall
Life doesn't frighten me at all
Bad dogs barking loud
Big ghosts in a cloud
Life doesn't frighten me at all.

Mean old Mother Goose
Lions on the loose
They don't frighten me at all
Dragons breathing flame
On my counterpane
That doesn't frighten me at all.

I go boo
Make them shoo
I make fun
Way they run
I won't cry
So they fly
I just smile
They go wild
Life doesn't frighten me at all.

Tough guys in a fight
All alone at night
Life doesn't frighten me at all.
Panthers in the park

Strangers in the dark
No, they don't frighten me at all.

That new classroom where
Boys all pull my hair
(Kissy little girls
With their hair in curls)
They don't frighten me at all.

Don't show me frogs and snakes
And listen for my scream.
If I'm afraid at all
It's only in my dreams.

I've got a magic charm
That I keep up my sleeve,
I can walk the ocean floor
And never have to breathe.

Life doesn't frighten me at all
Not at all
Not at all.
Life doesn't frighten me at all.

BUMP D'BUMP

Play me a game like Blind Man's dance
And bind my eyes with ignorance
Bump d'bump bump d'bump.

Tell my life with a liquor sign
Or a cooking spoon from the five-and-dime
And a junkie reel in two/four time
Bump d'bump bump d'bump.

Call me a name from an ugly south
Like liver lips and satchel mouth
Bump d'bump bump d'bump.

I'll play possum and close my eyes
To your greater sins and my lesser lies
That way I share my nation's prize
Bump d'bump bump d'bump.

I may be last in the welfare line
Below the rim where the sun don't shine
But getting up stays on my mind
Bump d'bump bump d'bump.

ON AGING

When you see me sitting quietly,
Like a sack left on the shelf,
Don't think I need your chattering.
I'm listening to myself.
Hold! Stop! Don't pity me!
Hold! Stop your sympathy!
Understanding if you got it,
Otherwise I'll do without it!

When my bones are stiff and aching
And my feet won't climb the stair,
I will only ask one favor:
Don't bring me no rocking chair.

When you see me walking, stumbling,
Don't study and get it wrong.
'Cause tired don't mean lazy
And every goodbye ain't gone.
I'm the same person I was back then,
A little less hair, a little less chin,
A lot less lungs and much less wind.
But ain't I lucky I can still breathe in.

IN RETROSPECT

Last year changed its seasons
subtly, stripped its sultry winds
for the reds of dying leaves, let
gelid drips of winter ice melt onto a
warming earth and urged the dormant
bulbs to brave the
pain of spring.

We, loving, above the whim of
time, did not notice.

Alone. I remember now.

JUST LIKE JOB

My Lord, My Lord,
Long have I cried out to Thee
In the heat of the sun,
The cool of the moon,
My screams searched the heavens for Thee.
My God,
When my blanket was nothing but dew,
Rags and bones
Were all I owned.
I chanted Your name
Just like Job.

Father, Father,
My life give I gladly to Thee
Deep rivers ahead
High mountains above
My soul wants only Your love
But fears gather round like wolves in the dark
Have You forgotten my name?
Oh, Lord, come to Your child.
Oh, Lord, forget me not.

You said to lean on Your arm
And I'm leaning
You said to trust in Your love
And I'm trusting
You said to call on Your name

And I'm calling
I'm stepping out on Your word.

You said You'd be my protection,
My only and glorious saviour
My beautiful Rose of Sharon,
And I'm stepping out on Your word.
Joy, joy
Your word.
Joy, joy
The wonderful word of the Son of God.

You said that You would take me to glory
To sit down at the welcome table
Rejoice with my mother in heaven
And I'm stepping out on Your word.

Into the alleys
Into the byways
Into the streets
And the roads
And the highways
Past rumor mongers
And midnight ramblers
Past the liars and the cheaters and the gamblers
On Your word
On Your word.
On the wonderful word of the Son of God.
I'm stepping out on Your word.

CALL LETTERS: MRS. V.B.

Ships?
Sure I'll sail them.
Show me the boat,
If it'll float,
I'll sail it.

Men?
Yes I'll love them.
If they've got the style,
To make me smile,
I'll love them.

Life?
'Course I'll live it.
Let me have breath,
Just to my death,
And I'll live it.

Failure?
I'm not ashamed to tell it,
I never learned to spell it.
Not Failure.

THANK YOU, LORD

———————— ⟫ ————————

I see You
Brown-skinned,
Neat Afro,
Full lips,
A little goatee.
A Malcolm,
Martin,
Du Bois.
Sunday services become sweeter when you're
    Black,
Then I don't have to explain why
I was out balling the town down,
Saturday night.

Thank You, Lord.
I want to thank You, Lord
For life and all that's in it.
Thank You for the day
And for the hour and for the minute.
I know many are gone,
I'm still living on,
I want to thank You.

I went to sleep last night
And I arose with the dawn,
I know that there are others
Who're still sleeping on,
They've gone away,

You've let me stay.
I want to thank You.

Some thought because they'd seen sunrise
They'd see it rise again.
But death crept into their sleeping beds
And took them by the hand.
Because of Your mercy,
I have another day to live.

Let me humbly say,
Thank You for this day
I want to thank You.

I was once a sinner man,
Living unsaved and wild,
Taking my chances in a dangerous world,
Putting my soul on trial.
Because of Your mercy,
Falling down on me like rain,
Because of Your mercy,
When I die I'll live again,
Let me humbly say,
Thank You for this day.
I want to thank You.

SHAKER,
WHY DON'T
YOU SING?

Another book for
GUY JOHNSON
and
COLIN ASHANTI MURPHY JOHNSON

Thanks to
ELEANOR TRAYLOR for her radiance
ELIZABETH PHILLIPS for her art
RUTH BECKFORD for her constancy

AWAKING IN NEW YORK

Curtains forcing their will
against the wind,
children sleep,
exchanging dreams with
seraphim. The city
drags itself awake on
subway straps; and
I, an alarm, awake as a
rumor of war,
lay stretching into dawn,
unasked and unheeded.

A GOOD WOMAN
FEELING BAD

The blues may be the life you've led
Or midnight hours in
An empty bed. But persecuting
Blues I've known
Could stalk
Like tigers, break like bone,

Pend like rope in
A gallows tree,
Make me curse
My pedigree,

Bitterness thick on
A rankling tongue,
A psalm to love that's
Left unsung,

Rivers heading north
But ending South,
Funeral music
In a going-home mouth.

All riddles are blues,
And all blues are sad,
And I'm only mentioning
Some blues I've had.

THE HEALTH-FOOD DINER

No sprouted wheat and soya shoots
And Brussels in a cake,
Carrot straw and spinach raw,
(Today, I need a steak).

Not thick brown rice and rice pilau
Or mushrooms creamed on toast,
Turnips mashed and parsnips hashed,
(I'm dreaming of a roast).

Health-food folks around the world
Are thinned by anxious zeal,
They look for help in seafood kelp
(I count on breaded veal).

No Smoking Signs, raw mustard greens,
Zucchini by the ton,
Uncooked kale and bodies frail
Are sure to make me run

to

Loins of pork and chicken thighs
And standing rib, so prime,
Pork chops brown and fresh ground round
(I crave them all the time).

Irish stews and boiled corned beef
and hot dogs by the scores,
or any place that saves a space
For smoking carnivores.

A GEORGIA SONG

We swallow the odors of Southern cities,
Fat back boiled to submission,
Tender evening poignancies of
Magnolia and the great green
Smell of fresh sweat.
In Southern fields,
The sound of distant
Feet running, or dancing,
And the liquid notes of
Sorrow songs,
Waltzes, screams and
French quadrilles float over
The loam of Georgia.

Sing me to sleep, Savannah.

Clocks run down in Tara's halls and dusty
Flags droop their unbearable
Sadness.

Remember our days, Susannah.

Oh, the blood-red clay,
Wet still with ancient
Wrongs, and Abenaa
Singing her Creole airs to
Macon.
We long, dazed, for winter evenings

And a whitened moon,
And the snap of controllable fires.

Cry for our souls, Augusta.

We need a wind to strike
Sharply, as the thought of love
Betrayed can stop the heart.
An absence of tactile
Romance, no lips offering
Succulence, nor eyes
Rolling, disconnected from
A Sambo face.

Dare us new dreams, Columbus.

A cool new moon, a
Winter's night, calm blood,
Sluggish, moving only
Out of habit, we need
Peace.

Oh Atlanta, oh deep, and
Once lost city,

Chant for us a new song. A song
Of Southern peace.

UNMEASURED TEMPO

The sun rises at midday.
Nubile breasts sag to waistlines while
young loins grow dull,
so late.
Dreams are petted, like
cherished lap dogs
misunderstood and loved
too well.

Much knowledge
wrinkles the cerebellum,
but little informs.
Leaps are
made into narrow mincings.
Great desires strain
into petty wishes.
You did arrive, smiling,
but too late.

AMOEBAEAN FOR DADDY

I was a pretty baby.
White folks used to stop
My mother
Just to look at me.
(All black babies
Are Cute.) Mother called me
Bootsie and Daddy said . . .
(Nobody listened to him).

On the Union Pacific, a
Dining-car waiter, bowing and scraping,
Momma told him to
Stand up straight, he shamed her
In the big house
(Bought from tips) in front of her
Nice club ladies.

His short legs were always
Half bent. He could have posed as
The Black jockey Mother found
And put on the lawn.
He sat silent when
We ate from the good railroad china
And stolen silver spoons.
Furniture crowded our
Lonely house.

But I was young and played
In the evenings under a blanket of
Licorice sky. When Daddy came home
(I might be forgiven) that last night,
I had been running in the
Big back yard and
Stood sweating above the tired old man,
Panting like a young horse,
Impatient with his lingering. He said
"All I ever asked, all I ever asked, all I ever—"
Daddy, you should have died
Long before I was a
Pretty baby, and white
Folks used to stop
Just to look at me.

RECOVERY

for Dugald

A last love,
proper in conclusion,
should snip the wings
forbidding further flight.

But I, now,
reft of that confusion,
am lifted up
and speeding toward the light.

IMPECCABLE CONCEPTION

I met a Lady Poet
who took for inspiration
colored birds, and whispered words,
a lover's hesitation.

A falling leaf could stir her.
A wilting, dying rose
would make her write, both day and night,
the most rewarding prose.

She'd find a hidden meaning
in every pair of pants,
then hurry home to be alone
and write about romance.

CAGED BIRD

A free bird leaps
on the back of the wind
and floats downstream
till the current ends
and dips his wing
in the orange sun rays
and dares to claim the sky.

But a bird that stalks
down his narrow cage
can seldom see through
his bars of rage
his wings are clipped and
his feet are tied
so he opens his throat to sing.

The caged bird sings
with a fearful trill
of things unknown
but longed for still
and his tune is heard
on the distant hill
for the caged bird
sings of freedom.

The free bird thinks of another breeze
and the trade winds soft through the sighing trees
and the fat worms waiting on a dawn-bright lawn
and he names the sky his own.

But a caged bird stands on the grave of dreams
his shadow shouts on a nightmare scream
his wings are clipped and his feet are tied
so he opens his throat to sing.

The caged bird sings
with a fearful trill
of things unknown
but longed for still
and his tune is heard
on the distant hill
for the caged bird
sings of freedom.

AVEC MERCI, MOTHER

From her perch of beauty
posing lofty,
Sustained upon the plaudits
of the crowd,

She praises all who kneel and
whispers softly,
"A genuflection's better
with head bowed."

Among the mass of people
who adore her
A solitary figure
holds her eyes.

His salty tears invoke
her sweet reaction,
"He's so much like his daddy
when he cries."

ARRIVAL

Angels gather.
The rush of mad air
cyclones through.
Wing tips brush the
hair, a million
strands
stand; waving black anemones.
Hosannahs crush the
shell's ear tender, and
tremble
down clattering
to the floor.
Harps sound,
undulate their
sensuous meanings.
Hallelujah! Hallelujah!
You
beyond the door.

A PLAGUED JOURNEY

There is no warning rattle at the door
nor heavy feet to stomp the foyer boards.
Safe in the dark prison, I know that
light slides over
the fingered work of a toothless
woman in Pakistan.
Happy prints of
an invisible time are illumined.
My mouth agape
rejects the solid air and
lungs hold. The invader takes
direction and
seeps through the plaster walls.
It is at my chamber entering
the keyhole, pushing
through the padding of the door.
I cannot scream. A bone
of fear clogs my throat.
It is upon me. It is
sunrise, with Hope
its arrogant rider.
My mind, formerly quiescent
in its snug encasement, is strained
to look upon their rapturous visages,
to let them enter even into me.
I am forced
outside myself to
mount the light and ride joined with Hope.

Through all the bright hours
I cling to expectation, until
darkness comes to reclaim me
as its own. Hope fades, day is gone
into its irredeemable place
and I am thrown back into the familiar
bonds of disconsolation.
Gloom crawls around
lapping lasciviously
between my toes, at my ankles,
and it sucks the strands of my
hair. It forgives my heady
fling with Hope. I am
joined again into its
greedy arms.

STARVATION

Hurray! Hurray!
Come through the keyhole.
Don't mind the rotting
sashes, pass into the windows.
Come, good news.

I'm holding my apron to
catch your plumpness.
The largest pot shines
with happiness. The slack
walls of my purse, pulsing
pudenda, await you with
a new bride's longing.
The bread bin gapes and
the oven holds its cold
breath.
Hurry up! Hurry down!
Good tidings. Don't wait
out my misery. Do not play
coy with my longing.

Hunger has grown old and
ugly with me. We hate from
too much knowing. Come.
Press out this sour beast which
fills the bellies of my children
and laughs at each eviction notice.
Come!

CONTEMPORARY ANNOUNCEMENT

Ring the big bells,
cook the cow,
put on your silver locket.
The landlord is knocking at the door
and I've got the rent in my pocket.

Douse the lights,
Hold your breath,
take my heart in your hand.
I lost my job two weeks ago
and rent day's here again.

PRELUDE TO A PARTING

Beside you, prone,
my naked skin finds
fault in touching.
Yet it is you
who draws away.
The tacit fact is:
the awful fear of losing
is not enough to cause
a fleeing love
to stay.

MARTIAL CHOREOGRAPH

Hello young sailor.
You are betrayed and
do not know the dance of death.
Dandy warrior, swaying to
Rick James on your
stereo, you do not hear the
bleat of triumphant war, its
roar is not in
your ears, filled with Stevie Wonder.

"Show me how to do like you.
Show me how to do it."

You will be surprised that
trees grunt when torn from
their root sockets to fandango into dust,
and exploding bombs force a lively Lindy
on grasses and frail bodies.

Go galloping on, bopping,
in the airport, young sailor.
Your body, virgin
still, has not swung the bloody buck and wing.

Manhood is a newly delivered
message. Your eyes,
rampant as an open city,
have not yet seen life steal from
limbs outstretched and trembling
like the arms of dancers
and dying swans.

TO A SUITOR

If you are Black and for me,
press steady, as the weight
of night. And I will show
cascades of brilliance, astrally.

If you are Black and constant,
descend importantly,
as ritual, and I will arch
a crescent moon, naturally.

INSOMNIAC

There are some nights when
sleep plays coy,
aloof and disdainful.
And all the wiles
that I employ to win
its service to my side
are useless as wounded pride,
and much more painful.

WEEKEND GLORY

Some dichty folks
don't know the facts,
posin' and preenin'
and puttin' on acts,
stretchin' their necks
and strainin' their backs.

They move into condos
up over the ranks,
pawn their souls
to the local banks.
Buying big cars
they can't afford,
ridin' around town
actin' bored.

If they want to learn how to live life right,
they ought to study me on Saturday night.

My job at the plant
ain't the biggest bet,
but I pay my bills
and stay out of debt.

I get my hair done
for my own self's sake,
so I don't have to pick
and I don't have to rake.

Take the church money out
and head cross town
to my friend girl's house
where we plan our round.
We meet our men and go to a joint
where the music is blues
and to the point.

Folks write about me.
They just can't see
how I work all week
at the factory.
Then get spruced up
and laugh and dance
And turn away from worry
with sassy glance.

They accuse me of livin'
from day to day,
but who are they kiddin'?
So are they.

My life ain't heaven
but it sure ain't hell.
I'm not on top
but I call it swell
if I'm able to work
and get paid right
and have the luck to be Black
on a Saturday night.

THE LIE

Today, you threaten to leave me.
I hold curses, in my mouth,
which could flood your path, sear
bottomless chasms in your road.

I keep, behind my lips,
invectives capable of tearing
the septum from your
nostrils and the skin from your back.

Tears, copious as a spring rain,
are checked in ducts
and screams are crowded in a corner
of my throat.

You are leaving?

Aloud, I say:
I'll help you pack, but it's getting late,
I have to hurry or miss my date.
When I return, I know you'll be gone.
Do drop a line or telephone.

PRESCIENCE

Had I known that the heart
breaks slowly, dismantling itself
into unrecognizable plots of
misery,

Had I known the heart would leak,
slobbering its sap, with a vulgar
visibility, into the dressed-up
dining rooms of strangers,

Had I known that solitude could
stifle the breath, loosen the joint,
and force the tongue against the
palate,

Had I known that loneliness could
keloid, winding itself around the
body in an ominous and beautiful
cicatrix,

Had I known yet I would have loved
you, your brash and insolent beauty,
your heavy comedic face
and knowledge of sweet
delights,

But from a distance
I would have left you whole and wholly
for the delectation of those who
wanted more and cared less.

FAMILY AFFAIRS

You let down, from arched
Windows,
Over hand-cut stones of your
Cathedrals, seas of golden hair.

While I, pulled by dusty braids,
Left furrows in the
Sands of African beaches.

Princes and commoners
Climbed over waves to reach
Your vaulted boudoirs,

As the sun, capriciously,
Struck silver fire from waiting
Chains, where I was bound.

My screams never reached
The rare tower where you
Lay, birthing masters for
My sons, and for my
Daughters, a swarm of
Unclean badgers, to consume
Their history.

Tired now of pedestal existence
For fear of flying
And vertigo, you descend
And step lightly over
My centuries of horror
And take my hand,

Smiling call me
  Sister.

Sister, accept
That I must wait a
While. Allow an age
Of dust to fill
Ruts left on my
Beach in Africa.

CHANGES

Fickle comfort steals away
What it knows
It will not say
What it can
It will not do
It flies from me
To humor you.

Capricious peace will not bind
The severed nerves
The jagged mind
The shattered dream
The loveless sleep
It frolics now
Within your keep.

Confidence, that popinjay,
Is planning now
To slip away
Look fast
It's fading rapidly
Tomorrow it returns to me.

BRIEF INNOCENCE

Dawn offers
innocence to a half-mad city.

The axe-keen
intent of all our
days for this brief
moment lies soft, nuzzling
the breast of morning,
crooning, still sleep-besotted,
of childish pranks with
angels.

THE LAST DECISION

The print is too small, distressing me.
Wavering black things on the page.
Wriggling polliwogs all about.
I know it's my age.
I'll have to give up reading.

The food is too rich, revolting me.
I swallow it hot or force it down cold,
and wait all day as it sits in my throat.
Tired as I am, I know I've grown old.
I'll have to give up eating.

My children's concerns are tiring me.
They stand at my bed and move their lips,
and I cannot hear one single word.
I'd rather give up listening.

Life is too busy, wearying me.
Questions and answers and heavy thought.
I've subtracted and added and multiplied,
and all my figuring has come to naught.
Today I'll give up living.

SLAVE COFFLE

Just Beyond my reaching,
    an itch away from fingers,
    was the river bed
    and the high road home.

Now Beneath my walking,
    solid down to China,
    all the earth is horror
    and the dark night long.

Then Before the dawning,
    bright as grinning demons,
    came the fearful knowledge
    that my life was gone.

SHAKER,
WHY DON'T YOU SING?

————————— ⌇ —————————

Evicted from sleep's mute palace,
I wait in silence
for the bridal croon;
your legs rubbing insistent
rhythm against my thighs,
your breast moaning
a canticle in my hair.
But the solemn moments,
unuttering, pass in
unaccompanied procession.
You, whose chanteys hummed
my life alive, have withdrawn
your music and lean inaudibly
on the quiet slope of memory.

O Shaker, why don't you sing?

In the night noisome with
street cries and the triumph
of amorous insects, I focus beyond
those cacophonies for
the anthem of your hands and swelling chest,
for the perfect harmonies which are
your lips. Yet darkness brings
no syncopated promise. I rest somewhere
between the unsung notes of night.

Shaker, why don't you sing?

MY LIFE HAS TURNED TO BLUE

Our summer's gone,
the golden days are through.
The rosy dawns I used to
wake with you
have turned to gray,
my life has turned to blue.

The once-green lawns
glisten now with dew.
Red robin's gone,
down to the South he flew.
Left here alone,
my life has turned to blue.

I've heard the news
that winter too will pass,
that spring's a sign
that summer's due at last.
But until I see you
lying in green grass,
my life has turned to blue.

ABOUT THE AUTHOR

MAYA ANGELOU, author of the bestselling *A Song Flung Up to Heaven, Even the Stars Look Lonesome, I Know Why the Caged Bird Sings, Gather Together in My Name, Singin' and Swingin' and Gettin' Merry Like Christmas, Wouldn't Take Nothing for My Journey Now* and the Oprah Book Club selection *The Heart of a Woman*, has also written five collections of poetry: *Just Give Me a Cool Drink of Water 'fore I Diiie; Oh Pray My Wings Are Gonna Fit Me Well; And Still I Rise; Shaker, Why Don't You Sing?* and *I Shall Not Be Moved*, as well as *On the Pulse of Morning*, which was read by her at the inauguration of President William Jefferson Clinton on January 20, 1993. In theater, she produced, directed and starred in *Cabaret for Freedom* in collaboration with Godfrey Cambridge at New York's Village Gate, starred in Genet's *The Blacks* at the St. Mark's Playhouse and adapted Sophocles' *Ajax*, which premiered at the Mark Taper Forum in Los Angeles in 1974. In film and television, she wrote the original screenplay and musical score for the film *Georgia, Georgia* and wrote and produced a ten-part TV series on African traditions in American life. In the sixties, at the request of Dr. Martin Luther King, Jr., she became Northern Coordinator for the Southern Christian Leadership Conference, and in 1975 she received the *Ladies' Home Journal* Woman of the Year Award in communications. She has received numerous honorary degrees, was appointed by

President Jimmy Carter to the National Commission on the Observance of International Women's Year and by President Gerald R. Ford to the American Revolution Bicentennial Advisory Council. She is on the board of trustees of the American Film Institute. One of the few female members of the Directors Guild, Angelou is the author of the television screenplays *I Know Why the Caged Bird Sings* and *The Sisters*. Most recently, she wrote the lyrics for the musical *King: Drum Major for Love* and was both host and writer for the series of documentaries *Maya Angelou's America: A Journey of the Heart*, along with Guy Johnson. Angelou is currently Reynolds Professor at Wake Forest University, Winston-Salem, North Carolina.

MAYA ANGELOU

I KNOW WHY THE CAGED BIRD SINGS

GATHER TOGETHER IN MY NAME

SINGIN' AND SWINGIN' AND GETTIN'
MERRY LIKE CHRISTMAS

THE HEART OF A WOMAN

MAYA ANGELOU: POEMS

WOULDN'T TAKE NOTHING FOR MY
JOURNEY NOW

I SHALL NOT BE MOVED

EVEN THE STARS LOOK LONESOME

Available from Bantam Books

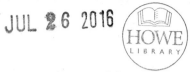